I0180913

HEAVEN'S HUG

Poems for God's Precious Children

DIANA YACOUB

HEAVEN'S HUG
Copyright © 2025 Diana Yacoub

All rights reserved. Neither this publication nor any part of this publication may be reproduced or transmitted in any form or by any means, electronic or mechanical, including photocopying, recording or any information storage and retrieval system, without permission in writing from the author.

This is a work of fiction. Names, characters, places and incidents either are the product of the author's imagination or are used fictitiously, and any resemblance to actual persons, living or dead, businesses, companies, events, or locales is entirely coincidental.

Scripture quotations taken from The Holy Bible, New International Version®, NIV®. Copyright © 1973, 1978, 1984, 2011 by Biblica, Inc. Used with permission of Zondervan. All rights reserved worldwide.
www.zondervan.com

Softcover ISBN: 978-1-4866-2747-9
Hardcover ISBN: 978-1-4866-2749-3
eBook ISBN: 978-1-4866-2748-6

WORD ALIVE
—PRESS—

Word Alive Press
119 De Baets Street, Winnipeg, MB R2J 3R9
www.wordalivepress.ca

Dear Jesus,
Thank You for loving every child, everywhere,
with a love that never let's go.
Wrap each one in Your arms,
so they always feel safe, seen, and special.
Let every heart know they are cherished by You—
wonderfully made, deeply known, and never forgotten.
I pray every child feels Your nearness
in quiet moments, in laughter, in tears and in dreams.
Keep them close, protect them always,
fill their hearts with peace,
and help them believe, always,
that everything You promise is true.
In Your name I pray,
Amen.

God's Love for Us

*For I am convinced that neither death nor life, neither angels nor demons,
neither the present nor the future, nor any powers, neither height nor depth,
nor anything else in all creation, will be able to separate us from
the love of God that is in Christ Jesus our Lord.*
Romans 8:38–39

No height too high, no sea too deep,
No scary night when we can't sleep.
No storm too strong, no place too far,
God's love will find us where we are.
Through every laugh, through every tear,
God holds us close, so do not fear.
His love will stay both bright and true
Forevermore for me and you!

God's Ultimate Love

For God so loved the world that he gave his one and only Son,
that whoever believes in him shall not perish but have eternal life.
John 3:16

God loved the world, the big and small.
He sent His Son to save us all!
Believe in Him, and you will see
A life with God eternally!
God loved the world so much, you see,
He sent His Son for you and me!
When we believe, our hearts are bright.
We'll live with Him in love and light!

You Are Beautiful

You are altogether beautiful, my darling; there is no flaw in you.
Song of Solomon 4:7

You are beautiful, don't you see?
God made you special, perfectly!
Not one mistake, so stand up tall.
You are His masterpiece, big or small.
You are precious, don't forget.
A sparkling gem—so lovely set.
No flaw is found, you're made just right.
A work of love, a joy, a light!

God's Perfect Timing

He has made everything beautiful in its time.
Ecclesiastes 3:11

God makes all things bright and new,
And that includes me and you!
He has a plan, just wait and see.
In His time, so beautifully!
He knows the perfect time to grow,
For seasons change and rivers flow.
God's plan is perfect, we can see.
He makes all things as they should be.

Made in God's Image

So God created mankind in his own image, in the image of God
he created them; male and female he created them.
Genesis 1:27

God made the stars, the sky so blue,
The flowers, the trees, and people too!
You're in His image, shining bright,
A precious child, a lovely sight!
We are His children, one and all,
Made with love, big and small.
You are special, this is true—
God made me, and God made you!

You Are on God's Heart

See, I have engraved you on the palms of my hands; your walls are ever before me.
Isaiah 49:16

God holds my name within His hand,
A love so deep, like golden sand.
No storm or wind can wash away
The love He shows me every day.
God wrote your name upon His hand,
A love so deep, forever planned.
He sees you always, day and night.
You are His joy, His heart's delight!

God Cares for You

When I consider your heavens, the work of your fingers, the moon and the stars, which you have set in place, what is mankind that you are mindful of them, human beings that you care for them?
Psalm 8:3-4

The stars at night, so high above,
Were made by God with lots of love!
But even greater is His care
For you, His child, beyond compare!
When I look up at the sky so high,
I see the stars and wonder why.
What are we, so small and sweet?
God loves us, His work elite!

You Are the Apple of God's Eye

For this is what the Lord Almighty says:
"...whoever touches you touches the apple of his eye..."
Zechariah 2:8

You are special, don't you know?
God watches over as you grow.
He calls you "precious" from on high,
The apple of His loving eye!
He says, "You're treasured to me, my dear.
I'll keep you safe, never fear.
In my love, you'll always stay,
Guided by me every day."

You Are Set Apart

Before I formed you in the womb I knew you, before you were born I set you apart...
Jeremiah 1:5

Before you were born, God knew your name,
He had a special plan, part of His great aim.
You're loved and known by God above,
Created with care, filled with His love!
God knew you before the start.
He made you special with a loving heart.
You are His treasure, unique and bright,
A precious creation, full of light!

You Are Wonderful

I praise you because I am fearfully and wonderfully made...
Psalm 139:14

My hands can clap, my feet can run,
I jump so high and have such fun!
God made me special, head to toe.
There's no one else like me, I know!
My heart can love, my voice can sing,
My life's a gift in everything.
God's masterpiece, so bright and true,
He made me, and He loves me too!

God's Love Never Ends

I have loved you with an everlasting love; I have drawn you with unfailing kindness.
Jeremiah 31:3

God's love for me is big and bright.
It shines like stars all through the night.
It never fades, it never goes,
It's warmer than the sun that glows.
No matter what, through thick and thin,
God's love will always pull me in.
Forever near, so kind and true,
"Dear child," He says, "I cherish you!"

God Sings over Me

The Lord your God is with you, the Mighty Warrior who saves.
He will take great delight in you; in his love he will no longer rebuke you,
but will rejoice over you with singing.
Zephaniah 3:17

God sings a song just for my heart,
A melody that won't depart.
His love is strong, His arms hold tight,
He watches over me at night.
With every step, He's by my side,
Through every tear, He's there to guide.
Oh what a joy, so sweet and free,
That God Himself sings over me!

www.ingramcontent.com/pod-product-compliance
Lightning Source LLC
LaVergne TN
LVHW072116070426
835510LV00002B/87